OXFORD

WILD READS

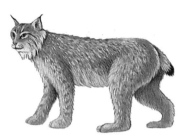

Big Cats

Kenneth Ireland

D1165954

OXFORD

UNIVERSITY PRESS

This book belongs to:

OXFORD
UNIVERSITY PRESS

Great Clarendon Street, Oxford OX2 6DP
Oxford University Press is a department of the University of Oxford.
It furthers the University's objective of excellence in research, scholarship,
and education by publishing worldwide in

Oxford   New York

Auckland Cape Town Dar es Salaam Hong Kong Karachi
Kuala Lumpur Madrid Melbourne Mexico City Nairobi
New Delhi Shanghai Taipei Toronto

With offices in

Argentina Austria Brazil Chile Czech Republic France Greece
Guatemala Hungary Italy Japan Poland Portugal Singapore
South Korea Switzerland Thailand Turkey Ukraine Vietnam

Oxford is a registered trade mark of Oxford University Press
in the UK and in certain other countries

Text © Kenneth Ireland
Illustrations © Claudia Saraceni
The moral rights of the author have been asserted

Database right Oxford University Press (maker)

This edition 2009

British Library Cataloguing in Publication Data

Data available

ISBN: 978-0-19-911925-7

1 3 5 7 9 10 8 6 4 2

Printed in China
Paper used in the production of this book is a natural,
recyclable product made from wood grown in sustainable forests.
The manufacturing process conforms to the environmental
regulations of the country of origin.

Contents

▶ What is a big cat?

Pet cats have soft fur, whiskers and claws. They can see very well at night. They can hear sounds a long way away. They meow and purr. They live with people who feed and look after them.

leopard

jaguar

cheetah

But what is a big cat?

Lions, tigers, leopards and jaguars
are big cats.

They have soft fur, whiskers and
claws too, but they are very
dangerous.

tiger

lion

They live in wild places in the world.
They have to hunt and kill other
animals for food.

Only their kittens meow and purr.
Big cats ROAR!

Did you know...
The kittens of a big cat are called cubs.

► King of the jungle

People call the lion "the king of the jungle" because it is so big and fierce.

Lions live together in a big family group called a pride. Once they lived in jungles in many places in the world. Now they live only in huge parks in Africa.

A male lion is longer than a small car. It is as heavy as three grown-ups put together.

It has long fur growing around its head. This is called a mane. It makes the lion look even more fierce.

a pride of lions

Did you know...
As a lion grows older its mane grows darker.

A pride of lions are hunting together.
The female lions have found a herd
of zebras and are hiding in the long
dry grass. Their fur is the same
colour as the grass so the zebras
cannot see them.

One female lion creeps round to the
other side of the herd. It moves
closer and closer. When the zebras
see it they start to run. But the other
female lions are waiting for them.

Did you know...
Lions hunt deer, antelopes, zebras and
many other animals.

They all suddenly pounce on one of
them. They hold it in their strong
claws.

They bite it with their sharp teeth.
Then the male lion runs in to join in
the feast!

Fearsome tiger

Tigers are very strong and fierce. They live in the forests and jungles of Asia. They usually hunt by themselves. They kill any large animals – even bears.

Tigers stalk through the long grass and among the trees. Because of their stripes, they can hardly be seen. They run or leap to catch their prey, then hold it in their claws and teeth.

Did you know...
Male tigers hunt to feed themselves. Female tigers hunt to feed themselves and their cubs.

All cats need to live near water so they can drink. But tigers are very good swimmers. And they love going into water just to cool off.

Tigers are nearly twice as long as most grown-ups. Some tigers are as heavy as four grown-ups put together! These are the biggest cats in the world.

tiger

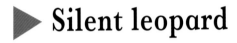

Silent leopard

Leopards live in Africa and Asia. They are the third biggest cats in the world.

They have tawny-coloured fur with lots of dark spots. This makes it hard for other animals to see them.

A leopard is hiding in a tree. It is watching and waiting. When an antelope comes along it leaps down on it. It is very strong. It kills the antelope with its sharp claws and teeth. Then it drags it back up the tree and into the branches.

Did you know...
A leopard with completely black fur is called a panther. When these hunt at night they cannot be seen at all!

Snow leopards are smaller than ordinary leopards. They live in cold snowy places in Asia. Their pale thick fur with smudgy-looking spots keeps out the cold.

They can leap many times their own length.

snow leopard

Clouded leopards live in the forests of Asia. They are long and thin.

They climb trees so fast they can even catch birds. But mostly they hunt on the ground.

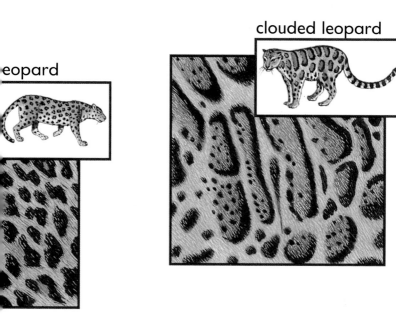

clouded leopard

eopard

You can see why they are called clouded leopards.

▶ Solitary jaguar

Jaguars are the biggest cats in Central and South America. They look rather like leopards but their spots have smaller spots inside them.

Jaguars are strong and deadly hunters. Like leopards, they are very good climbers. Like leopards they sometimes leap down on other animals from rocks and trees.

Jaguars also like to keep close to water. There they sometimes catch fish in their claws. Cubs learn how to do this while they are playing.

jaguar

▶ Speedy cheetah

Cheetahs are the fastest animals on earth. They can run almost as fast as a car on a motorway.

Cheetahs are long and slim. They have powerful legs, a long tail and a small head. They can chase antelopes and gazelles for up to three miles but they usually give up long before then.

cheetah

Like lions, they hunt mainly in the daytime.

Once, cheetahs lived in most parts of Asia and Africa. But now a few thousand are left only in Africa.

cheetah

Did you know...
Cheetahs are the only cats which cannot hide their claws.

Some other big cats

Although these are still big cats, they are rather smaller. The first three all live in North America.

Bobcat

Bobcats are often found in a tree or lying on rocks. They catch other animals by jumping on them or chasing them.

bobcat

Lynx

A lynx looks like a bobcat but with tufts of hair on its ears. They are also found in Sweden, Finland and Spain.

lynx

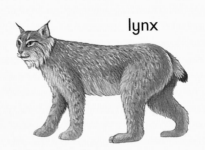

Puma

Pumas spend most of their time in trees. They can jump very high. They are also called mountain lions and cougars.

puma

Ocelot

Ocelots live in South American forests. They often make their dens in hollow trees. They are about the size of pet cats but very dangerous.

ocelot

Pampas cat

Pampas cats live mostly in the big plains of South America called pampas. They are not much bigger than pet cats. Their pale fur with dark stripes and spots often has a mane along the back.

pampas cat

Caracal

Caracals live in the deserts of Africa and Asia. They have long ears with tufts of hair on the end. They often kill lizards and small snakes.

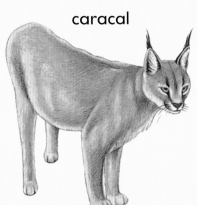

caracal

Serval

Servals live among the tall grasses, bushes and trees of Africa. They usually eat small animals and birds, but are strong enough to kill antelopes.

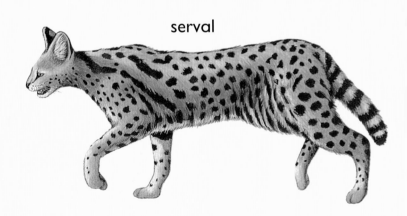

serval

Golden cat

African golden cats are nearly a metre long with a long tail. Indian golden cats are bigger with a white stripe on their face. These can even kill buffalo calves.

golden cat

Wild cat

Wild cats live in the mountains of Europe. They might look like big pet cats but they are dangerous. They sleep during the day and hunt at night.

wild cat

 # But ...

Each year there are fewer and fewer big cats left in the world. So what has happened to them?

Many have been killed because people were scared of them. Forests and jungles have been cut down. Then big cats have nowhere to hunt, so they starve.

100 years ago, there were about 100,000 tigers living in the wild. Now there are fewer than 7,000.

Will there be any big cats left in the world in another 100 years time?

▶ Glossary

 antelopes and gazelles
These are both a kind of deer.
11, 17, 22, 26

 herd A herd is a group of animals living and feeding together.
9, 10

 hunt When animals hunt, they are looking for other animals to eat.
6, 9, 11, 12, 13, 17, 19, 23, 27

 pampas Big wide plains with not many trees in South America are called pampas.
25

pounce When a big cat pounces, it attacks suddenly, usually by jumping.   **11**

 prey Prey is any animal that another animal wants to eat.

13

 stalk Stalking is when an animal creeps quietly, usually to take something by surprise.

13

OXFORD

WILD READS

WILD READS will help your child develop a love of reading and a lasting curiosity about our world. See the websites and places to visit below to learn more about big cats.

Big Cats

WEBSITES
http://www.thebigcats.com/

Fun facts, games and quizzes
http://www.wwf.org.uk/gowild/

http://www.bbc.co.uk/cbbc/wild/amazinganimals/

PLACES TO VISIT
Longleat Safari Park
http://www.longleat.co.uk/

Isle of Wight Zoo
http://www.isleofwightzoo.com/
Visit the tiger sanctuary to see one of the largest collections of tigers in Europe.

West Midlands Safari and Leisure Park
http://www.wmsp.co.uk/index.php
Visit a family of white tigers!